AUG   2005

The Dust Bowl

by Ann Heinrichs

Content Adviser: Dr. Alan Rogers, History Department Chair,
Boston College, Boston, Massachusetts

Reading Adviser: Susan Kesselring, M.A., Literacy Educator,
Rosemount-Apple Valley-Eagan (Minnesota) School District

COMPASS POINT BOOKS
MINNEAPOLIS, MINNESOTA

Compass Point Books
3109 West 50th Street, #115
Minneapolis, MN 55410

Visit Compass Point Books on the Internet at *www.compasspointbooks.com*
or e-mail your request to *custserv@compasspointbooks.com*

On the cover: A dust storm strikes Rolla, Kansas, in May 1935.

Photographs ©: Franklin D. Roosevelt Library, cover, 5, 19; Prints Old and Rare, back cover (far left);
Library of Congress, back cover, 8, 14, 18, 23, 24, 27, 31, 34, 37, 38, 39, 41; Arthur Rothstein/Library of
Congress/Time Life Pictures/Getty Images, 4, 13; Sloan/USDA, 7; North Wind Picture Archives, 9; Courtesy
Scotts Bluff National Monument, 10; Stock Montage, 11, 15, 26, 36; DVIC/Sgt. Leon H. Caverly, 12; Loomis
Dean/Time Life Pictures/Getty Images, 16; B. C. McLean/Three Lions/Getty Images, 17; Michael
Rougier/Time Life Pictures/Getty Images, 21; B.C. McLean/USDA, 22; American Stock/Getty Images, 25;
Three Lions/Getty Images, 28; Marion Post Wolcott/USDA, 30; Hulton Archive/Getty Images, 32; Dorothea
Lange/Resettlement Administration/Time Life Pictures/Getty Images, 33; Keystone/Getty Images, 40.

Creative Director: Terri Foley
Managing Editor: Catherine Neitge
Editor: Brenda Haugen
Photo Researcher: Marcie C. Spence
Designer/Page production: Bradfordesign, Inc./Les Tranby
Educational Consultant: Diane Smolinski
Cartographer: XNR Productions, Inc.

Library of Congress Cataloging-in-Publication Data
Heinrichs, Ann.
   The dust bowl / by Ann Heinrichs.
      p. cm. — (We the people)
Includes bibliographical references and index.
Audience: Grades 4-6.
ISBN 0-7565-0837-1 (hardcover)
1. Dust Bowl Era, 1931-1939—Juvenile literature. 2. Great Plains—History—20th century—Juvenile
literature. 3. Agriculture—Great Plains—History—20th century—Juvenile literature. 4. Farmers—Great
Plains—Social conditions—20th century—Juvenile literature. I. Title. II. We the people (Series) (Compass
Point Books)
F595.H45 2005
978'.033—dc22   2004016719

TABLE OF CONTENTS

"The Saddest Land I Have Ever Seen"

"If you would like to have your heart broken, just come out here. . . . This is the dust-storm country. It is the saddest land I have ever seen."

—News reporter Ernie Pyle, 1936

A father and his sons battle the wind and dirt to walk toward a shack in 1936.

4

Blinding dust storms whipped across the heartland of the United States in the 1930s. The storms blew tons of rich soil off the fields. Millions of acres of farmland were destroyed. Dead cattle and ruined tractors lay half-buried in the dust. Hundreds of thousands of farmers packed up and left their homes. This sad scene was in a region that became known as the Dust Bowl.

A dust storm in Amarillo, Texas

5

The Dust Bowl covered the southern part of the Great Plains. This is a vast area in the center of the United States. It includes Kansas, Oklahoma, Colorado, New Mexico, and Texas. The damage from dust storms also reached into Arkansas, Nebraska, Wyoming, Montana, North Dakota, and South Dakota—making this one of the nation's worst disasters.

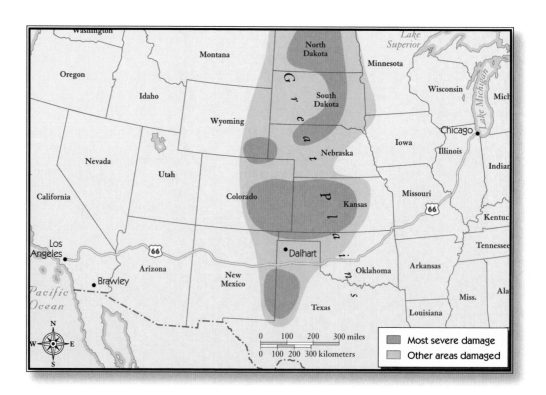

The Dust Bowl era was called the Dirty '30s. It lasted through most of the 1930s. Before this time, the soil had been overused by farmers. Planting the same crop year after year wears out soil. Then a terrible drought struck the Great Plains. The soil became dry and dusty. One after another, dust storms blasted across the plains. They simply blew dry soil off the fields.

The soil blew into houses, barns, and other farm buildings. It covered fences, farm machines, cars, and furniture. It often was so deep, the soil had to be shoveled out of buildings

Dirt buries machinery in Dallas, South Dakota, in 1936.

7

and away from machinery. Some Dust Bowl farmers packed up and left. Others stayed and tried to continue farming. Whichever choice they made, no one had it easy. The Dust Bowl was a heartbreaking experience for all.

Oklahoma Dust Bowl refugees living out of their car in 1935

8

WHY FARMS FAILED

"Harvesting wheat was a thrill to me. . . . It was breathtaking—hundreds of acres of wheat that were mine. To me it was the most beautiful scene in all the world."

—Lawrence Svobida, Kansas wheat farmer

Grasslands once covered the Great Plains. Before white settlers arrived, these grasslands were rich hunting grounds. Native Americans hunted the herds of buffalo that grazed there.

In the mid-1800s, Plains Indians rode horses when they hunted buffalo.

9

The grasslands were more than just animal food. The grasses and their roots protected the soil. They held it in place through wind and rain. The grasses also trapped nutrients and rainwater. This kept the soil rich and moist.

Pioneer farmers began pouring into the Great Plains in the early 1800s. They were thrilled to find such fine, black soil. The soil was so rich, one farmer said it looked like chocolate.

A wagon train brings settlers to open land in the Great Plains.

The topsoil was the most fertile. As old plants rotted, they added nutrients to the soil. It had taken hundreds of years to build up that layer of topsoil. Farmers plowed up the grasses and planted wheat and other crops in that rich earth.

In Kansas, Native Americans warned some farmers to leave the grass in place. Yet the harvests were so bountiful, farmers could not resist clearing more land.

"It looked like it was just a thing that would never end," a Texas farmer said. The lush, green grasslands seemed to go on forever. So did the soil.

Some settlers used teams of oxen to help clear land and make it suitable for farming.

11

During World War I (1914–1918), farm production increased. The nation needed tons of wheat and beef to feed its troops. Farmers were getting high prices for their products because these items were in demand. After the war, though, the products were no longer in such demand, so the price of farm products dropped. Suddenly, farmers and ranchers were making less money. They were desperate. They needed money to pay their mortgages and buy seeds, fertilizer, and many other important things. What could they do?

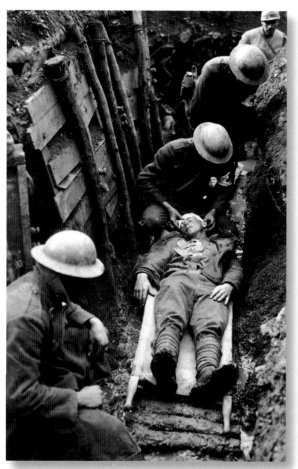

A Marine receives first aid during World War I.

12

Soil erosion in Chilton County, Alabama, in 1937

For farmers on the "endless" plains, the answer was easy. They simply cleared more grassland for farming. They also bought mechanical farm equipment to make the work faster and easier.

Before the 1930s, farmers were using horse-drawn plows. They could turn over about 3 acres (1.2 hectares) of land a day. However, a tractor could plow about 50 acres (20 hectares) a day! Now farmers could grow more crops than ever before.

Ranchers stepped up their businesses, too. They enlarged their herds and grazed them over bigger areas.

All this activity was hard on the land. The roots of grass had once held the soil in place. Plowing and grazing tore up the roots and left the soil loose and dry. Soil erosion started to happen. That is, the topsoil began to disappear. Little by little, wind and rain were sweeping it away.

No one could have predicted the disaster that struck next. It began on "Black Tuesday"—October 29, 1929. That was the day the stock market crashed.

People buy shares of stock with the hope that the value of the shares will increase. Then, if they later sell their shares, they will make a profit. On Black Tuesday, share prices fell about 80 percent. This meant if a person bought one share that was worth $1 the day before, on Black Tuesday it was only worth 20 cents. When the price of the shares fell, people panicked and tried to get whatever they could for their shares. A record 16,410,030 shares were sold on Black Tuesday, and thousands of people lost huge amounts of money.

The New York Times ran a story about the record numbers of shares sold the day before.

14

An Iowa bank closed during the Depression.

People lost faith in the economy. Many saved the money they had and quit buying goods and services they would have bought before the crash. As a result, many factories and businesses closed. Millions of people lost their jobs.

With people unable to repay their loans, many banks across the country closed, too. Some people had their life's savings in banks. In one day, they lost every penny they had saved in these banks. The entire country entered a period called the Great Depression.

Farmers continued to work on their farms. Yet, many were in debt. They had borrowed money to buy farm machines. Now they had lost their savings, too. When bankers came to collect on the debts, many farmers could not pay. If a farmer could not pay, the bank would take back the farm or the equipment as payment.

Poor farming practices leave this field dry and cracked. Salt collects where water ran off the field instead of seeping into it.

A sandstorm hits a Texas farm in 1938.

To make matters worse, the Great Plains suffered a serious drought. Beginning in 1931, very little rain fell upon the plains. The drought lasted for eight long years. Even if crops came up, they soon shriveled and died.

"[We] went 72 days without a drop of rain, and everything just burned up," an Oklahoma farmer remembered. One woman recalled her girlhood days during the drought: "Our corn got two feet high and burned to pieces in the field."

Cattle died, too, because they had nothing to eat. The once-rich soil became parched and sandy. When the dust storms set in, the dried-up farm soil just blew away.

17

BLACK BLIZZARDS

Our relatives were huddled into their oil boom shacks,

And the children they was cryin' as it whistled through the cracks.

And the family it was crowded into their little room,

They thought the world had ended, and they thought it

was their doom.

—From "Dust Storm Disaster" by Woody Guthrie

A large oak tree is cut down by a Missouri farmer in 1938.

A black blizzard strikes South Dakota in 1934.

Farmers on the Great Plains had often struggled with dust storms. In the 1930s, though, the storms were especially fierce. Trees, bushes, and grasses had all been cleared. There was nothing to break the force of the wind. It blasted across the plains, sweeping tons of dry soil into the sky.

People called the dust storms black blizzards. The dust swirled up in huge black clouds. "You couldn't even tell where the sun was," a farm woman recalled.

There were 14 dust storms in 1932 and 38 dust storms in 1933. A terrible storm blew across the plains in May 1934. It picked up about 350 million tons (318 million metric tons) of soil. The clouds of gritty dirt kept on blowing eastward. Within days, they had blown all the way to the East Coast of the United States!

The "Black Sunday" storm on April 14, 1935, was the worst of them all. That day started clear and sunny. However, in the afternoon a black cloud appeared in the distance. It moved so fast, birds couldn't fly out of its path. Day turned to night as the cloud blocked out the sun. Many people thought the world was ending. The storm struck eastern Colorado, Kansas, Oklahoma, and Texas.

Spring was the season for dust storms. Usually, this was a time of fresh hope for new growth. Farmers had plowed the soil, made neat rows of furrows, and planted their seeds. They had watched and waited, day after day, for the first signs of growth. Finally, leafy shoots of wheat began to pop up out of the soil. Then the winds would came.

Hit by the blasts of wind, the new shoots were not strong enough to hold their own in the ground. Gusts of wind ripped the plants out by the roots. Farmers saw their weeks of labor torn apart in one day.

Crops dry up in a Texas field during the Dust Bowl.

A farmstead is damaged by drifting sand in Dallas County, Texas, in 1938.

The farmers lost more than their crops. They also lost their soil. When powerful winds whipped across the plains, they easily swept the topsoil away.

Anyone caught in a dust storm had a frightful time. The stinging, windswept dust felt like pinpricks on a person's skin.

"The impact is like a shovelful of fine sand flung against the face," a reporter wrote. A Kansas farmer said the wind "caused my face to blister so that the skin peeled off." Dust blew into people's eyes. It filled their mouths and choked their lungs.

Indoors, people nailed wet sheets and blankets over their windows and doors. They even sat with wet cloths over their faces to keep the dirt out.

The windows in this home in Williams County, North Dakota, are sealed to keep the dust out.

Still, many babies and old people died from breathing in so much dirt. Doctors called it "dust pneumonia."

No matter how tightly people sealed up their homes, dirt blew inside. It got into the water and the food. It filled every crack.

Ann Marie Low was a North Dakota farm girl at the time. She wrote about the dust in her *Dust Bowl Diary:*

"[The dirt] sifts into everything. After we wash the dishes and put them away, so much dirt sifts into the cupboards we must wash them again before the next meal. Clothes in the closets are covered with dust. Last weekend no one was taking an automobile out for fear of ruining the motor."

The American Red Cross began issuing dust masks. Children wore them to school. Farmers wore them in the fields. People were brokenhearted to see what the dust did to their pets and farm animals. Some were blinded by the dust. Others died because they couldn't breathe. Their lungs had filled with dust.

An Arkansas farmer puts on a mask to keep from breathing in dust.

A South Dakota home is covered with dirt up to its roof after a 1934 storm.

Dust piled up like snowdrifts against houses and barns. Some drifts even covered entire buildings. People had to shovel the dust out of their homes. In the worst of times, schools and hospitals closed. Normal life simply could not keep going.

OKIES AND HOBO BRATS

Car-loads, caravans, homeless and hungry, twenty thousand and fifty thousand and a hundred thousand and two hundred thousand. They streamed over the mountains, hungry and restless—restless as ants, scurrying to find work to do.

— From *The Grapes of Wrath* by John Steinbeck

Dust Bowl farmers packed their belongings and headed west during the Depression.

A migrant worker's family in Nipomo, California, in 1936

Their farms in ruins, thousands of farmers gave up. They loaded everything they could into their trucks and cars. Tables, chairs, and mattresses were piled high. Then the farmers took off, many heading west on Route 66. Their destination? California!

Mildred Ward left Oklahoma for California in 1938. She and her family had lots of company along the way.

"Oh, the road was just full of people like us coming out here. People with all their belongings tied onto old cars . . . and even on tops of their cars. Cars full of kids— most of them had big families of kids," she said.

Workers leave the field with bags full of cotton in Kern County, California.

To many Dust Bowl victims, California seemed like the perfect place. They could get jobs working as migrants on California's many farms. California had a mild climate and plenty of farmland. Farmers there could grow a variety of crops. By planting different crops at different times, they could get several harvests each year. The migrants hoped they could buy their own farms by saving what they earned working on other people's farms.

28

As it turned out, California was not the perfect place after all. The state had nowhere to put all the newcomers. In 1937, California passed a law closing its borders to outsiders. Thousands of migrant families were met by armed guards at the state's border. It would be four years before the U.S. Supreme Court would overturn this law.

If the migrants who did make it in expected to be welcomed, they were sadly mistaken. Native Californians looked down on the new arrivals. Only about one out of five migrants was from Oklahoma. However, Californians called all the migrants Okies. The Okies were seen as ignorant, dirty, and even dangerous.

"[P]eople felt that we were dumb, ignorant," said one migrant mother. "In fact, when our son started to school here he came home several times and told me the kids had called him a dumb Okie . . . and he didn't even know what an Okie was."

There were far too many migrant workers and not enough work. For those who did work, wages were very low.

A family works together to pick beans in a field.

Parents, children, and old folks all worked long hours in the fields. Still, many families did not make enough money to live.

Homeless families camped out by roadsides and irrigation ditches. Those ditches were their only water supplies.

Conditions in the camps were unclean and unhealthy. Local hospitals often took in migrants with typhoid, dysentery, and other diseases.

None of the workers could really settle down in one place. Farms in different regions grew many different types of crops. Lettuce grew in one area, oranges in another, and cotton somewhere else. All these crops ripened at different times. As soon as one harvest was complete, it was time to move on to another.

Many sad songs were written during this time. Folk singer Woody Guthrie gave voice to people's pain and despair. A migrant from Oklahoma himself, he knew these feelings firsthand.

Woody Guthrie

31

John Steinbeck

Author John Steinbeck wrote the novel *The Grapes of Wrath*. It's a heartbreaking tale about the Joad family's move from Oklahoma to California. When the book was made into a movie, people around the country shared the sorrows of the migrants' lives.

Dorothea Lange told the migrants' story another way. As a photographer, she captured many pitiful scenes of the time. Her subjects ranged from wiped-out farms to hungry children. Lange's photos caught the attention of the government. Her work led to better housing for California's migrants.

The Farm Security Administration (FSA) began building camps for migrant workers in 1937. People in Brawley, California, were angry about the camp in their

An Oklahoma family of migrant potato harvesters eats supper in California in 1935.

town. Members of the parent-teacher association made nasty comments: "Are you going to make it possible for more of these hobo brats to go to school with our children?" The migrants were good students, though. After life on the road and in the fields, they welcomed the chance to be in school.

Dozens of migrant camps soon stretched through California's farming country. The camps provided tents, showers, toilets, and child care. They also gave migrants a place where they could feel safe from unfriendly locals.

Camp residents formed councils to discuss problems and organize activities. In the evenings, they played cards

33

An FSA migrant camp in Brawley, California, gave children lots of room to play.

and checkers. They relaxed, sang songs, and told stories after their long day's work. At last they could share a real sense of community.

34

TOO STUBBORN TO LEAVE

"Every dime I got is tied up right here. . . . I know what the land did once for me; maybe it will do it again."
—Farmer in Dalhart, Texas

Leaving was one solution to the Dust Bowl horror. Another solution was staying home. Back on the Great Plains, thousands of people stayed behind. They just did the best they could.

There were many reasons for staying. Some people couldn't afford to move. They had no money to live on while getting resettled. Some people had no car. They didn't want to haul their household goods to California by horse-drawn wagon. Some people simply loved their patch of land, no matter what. It was home. Finally, some people were just too stubborn to leave. They refused to let hardship get the best of them.

35

Staying on the farms was tough. After the worst of the dust storms, farmers faced huge cleanup jobs. They had to level their fields again so they could start planting. There were mountains of piled-up dirt to smooth out. For some farmers, it was just too much to handle. They left their farms and hunted for jobs.

Franklin D. Roosevelt tried to help. He became president in 1933. Both the Great Depression and the Dust Bowl disaster occurred while he was in office. To aid his suffering countrymen, Roosevelt introduced his New Deal program. It set up agencies that gave people, including some farmers, steady jobs and helped them earn money.

The Works Progress Administration built bridges,

Franklin D. Roosevelt

highways, and dams.
The Civilian
Conservation Corps
built national parks,
camps, and trails. The
government also helped
get food and money to
farmers who didn't take
other jobs. Many hated
to take handouts, but
they had no choice.

The Soil
Conservation Service
(SCS) was a great help to

Members of the Civilian Conservation Corps build steps at a picnic ground in Ohio.

farmers, too. Its first director, Hugh Bennett, is called the father of soil conservation. SCS workers taught people new farming methods to protect the land. One new practice was contour farming. Farmers usually planted their crops in straight rows. With contour farming, they plowed in wavy lines, following curves in the land.

37

Strip farming involves planting strips of different kinds of crops next to one another and following the contour of the land.

Another practice was terracing. This was planting crops on several levels, like the steps of stairs. Strip farming and no-till farming were some other new tricks. All these methods cut down on soil erosion.

Farmers also were encouraged to plant trees on their farms. Trees would trap moisture and hold the soil in place. In addition, they would break the force of the winds. The government planted more than 200 million trees from North Dakota to Texas. The rows of trees were called shelter belts.

Many farmers resisted the new farming methods. As one farmer said, "Most of these old-timers wouldn't do it." Then the government started paying people to change. The farmers finally caught on: "You could make a dollar an acre if you practiced one of these methods." Though the drought continued, recovery was on the way.

AFTER THE DUST BOWL

"When the rain came, it meant life itself. . . . And we as young people . . . you'd go out in that rain and just feel that rain hit your face."
—Floyd Coen, Dust Bowl survivor

The long dry spell ended in the autumn of 1939. Rain drenched the plains for two days and nights. Rainfall returned to normal, and farmers enjoyed "heavenly rains" in the early 1940s. Once again, stalks of golden wheat waved across the plains.

Rain falls over New Mexico in September 1939.

A field of wheat in Indiana is almost ready to be harvested.

"People are thinking differently about taking care of the land," said a Kansas farmer. That care paid off in the years to come. Droughts struck the Great Plains again in the 1950s and the 1980s. Yet the effects were never as severe as they were during the 1930s.

Life improved for the Dust Bowl migrants in California in the 1940s, too. In 1941, the United States entered World War II (1939–1945). Many new factories opened up to provide war supplies. Victims of the Dust Bowl disaster now had new opportunities. Some got jobs in these factories making uniforms, weapons, or warships. Others signed up to fight in the war.

The war changed the way Californians felt about their migrant neighbors. On the battlefield, personal differences no longer mattered. "Over there, there was no room for being stuck up," a Californian said. The soldiers "would just as soon have an Okie save their life as anybody. … We became equal. … We were all on common ground."

A mechanic in an aircraft plant rivets the belly of a plane during World War II.

41

GLOSSARY

dysentery—a disease that causes severe diarrhea with the passing of blood and mucus

erosion—the wearing away of soil by wind and water

furrows—grooves in the soil made by a plow

Great Depression—an era of severe unemployment and poverty in the United States that began with the October 1929 stock market crash; it lasted throughout the 1930s and was relieved by America's entry into World War II

hobo—a homeless person who travels from place to place

stock market—a system in which stocks and shares in companies are bought and sold

typhoid—a serious disease caused by germs in water or food

DID YOU KNOW?

- The "Black Sunday" dust cloud moved about 60 miles (97 kilometers) an hour.

- About 2.5 million people left the Great Plains during the Dust Bowl era. About 200,000 of them moved to California.

- The Farm Security Administration built 13 migrant camps in California. Each one housed about 300 families.

- Three out of four Dust Bowl farmers chose to stay on their farms instead of migrating to other states.

- Droughts occurred in the 1730s, the 1820s, and the 1860s. However, the 1930s drought was the longest and most severe.

- Photographs taken by Dorothea Lange during the Dust Bowl years are found in this book on pages 27 and 33.

IMPORTANT DATES

Timeline

1931 — A drought, which ends up lasting for years, hits the Great Plains.

1932 — The "black blizzard" dust storms begin.

1933 — The Emergency Farm Mortgage Act and the Farm Credit Act keep many from losing their farms.

1934 — The drought now affects more than three-fourths of the country; a dust storm in May blows dust from the Great Plains to the East Coast.

1935 — The "Black Sunday" dust storm takes place on April 14; the U.S. government establishes the Drought Relief Service, the Soil Conservation Service, the Works Progress Administration, and other helpful agencies.

1937 — The Farm Security Administration opens the first of its migrant worker camps in California.

1939 — Rains begin to fall again in the autumn, ending the long period of drought.

IMPORTANT PEOPLE

HUGH H. BENNETT (1881-1960)
First director of the Soil Conservation Service; called the father of soil conservation

WOODY GUTHRIE (1912-1967)
Folksinger and composer whose songs tell of Americans' hardships in the 1930s

DOROTHEA LANGE (1895-1965)
Photographer who took dramatic pictures of victims of the Great Depression and the Dust Bowl disaster

FRANKLIN D. ROOSEVELT (1882-1945)
U.S. president whose New Deal programs relieved much of the nation's poverty and unemployment during the Great Depression

JOHN STEINBECK (1902-1968)
Author whose novel The Grapes of Wrath *showed the horrors of migrant life*

WANT TO KNOW MORE?

At the Library

Durbin, William. *The Journal of C. J. Jackson: A Dust Bowl Migrant.* New
York: Scholastic, 2002.

Heinrichs, Ann. *California.* Minneapolis: Compass Point Books, 2003.

Hesse, Karen. *Out of the Dust.* New York: Scholastic Press, 1997.

Stanley, Jerry. *Children of the Dust Bowl: The True Story of the School at
Weedpatch Camp.* New York: Crown, 1992.

Turner, Ann Warren. *Dust for Dinner.* New York: HarperCollins, 1995.

On the Web

For more information on the *Dust Bowl,* use FactHound

to track down Web sites related to this book.

1. Go to *www.facthound.com.*

2. Type in a search word related to this book

or this book ID: 0756508371.

3. Click on the *Fetch It* button.

Your trusty FactHound will fetch the best Web sites for you!

On the Road

Cimarron Heritage Center

1300 N. Cimarron

Boise City, OK 73933

580/544-3497

To learn about the region's history, including the Dust Bowl years

Oakland Museum of California

1000 Oak St.

Oakland, CA 94607

510/238-2200

To see the country's largest collection of Dorothea Lange photos from the Dust Bowl era

Look for more We the People books about this era:

The Dust Bowl

Ellis Island

The Great Depression

Industrial America

Navajo Code Talkers

Pearl Harbor

The Persian Gulf War

The Statue of Liberty

The Titanic

The Tuskegee Airmen

A complete list of We the People titles is available on our Web site:
www.compasspointbooks.com

INDEX

About the Author

Ann Heinrichs was born in Fort Smith, Arkansas, and now lives in Chicago, Illinois. Some of her "Arkie" relatives moved to California over the years, though her immediate family stayed home. Ann is the author of more than 100 books for children and young adults. In researching her books, she has traveled widely throughout the United States, Europe, Africa, and the Middle East.